The
Happy
Broadcast

ANXIETY-FREE NEWS!

First published in North America by The Unnamed Press
www.unnamedpress.com
Unnamed Press, and the colophon, are registered trademarks of Unnamed Media LLC.

US ISBN: 978-1-95121-316-9   US eISBN: 978-1-951213-17-6
Catalog-in-data information is available upon request.
Distributed in North America by Publishers Group West

First published in the UK in 2020 by Studio Press,
an imprint of Bonnier Books UK,
The Plaza, 535 King's Road, London SW10 0SZ
www.studiopressbooks.co.uk
www.bonnierbooks.co.uk

UK ISBN 978-1-78741-770-0   UK eISBN 978-1-78741-864-6
A CIP catalogue for this book is available from the British Library

© 2020 The Happy Broadcast

Created, designed and illustrated by Mauro Gatti
Edited by Sophie Blackman
Typeset by Jaya Nicely

1 3 5 7 9 10 8 6 4 2
Printed and bound in China

Hello there!

WHAT IS
The Happy Broadcast ?

Ciao, I'm Mauro Gatti, the author of this book and creator of The Happy Broadcast.

In 2018, I decided to use my talents as a designer to spread some positivity by highlighting the good happening in the world.

That day, The Happy Broadcast was born as an online source for positive news, highlighting the importance of mental health and sustainability.

Since then, it has become a trusted place for both adults and children to find positive, fact-checked news stories. With suggestions of how to get involved, these stories are intended to inspire you to make the world just a little bit better in your own community.

Sometimes the world seems so full of problems
that we feel overwhelmed, afraid, or alone.

NEGATIVE NEWS GIVES US THE IMPRESSION THAT THERE IS NO GOOD LEFT IN THE WORLD.

We might feel helpless watching terrible events unfold.

BUT IGNORING THE BAD NEWS DOESN'T WORK FOR ME.

I don't want to be a victim of unrealistic optimism.

I want to look for solutions to problems and focus on what I am able to do. I am inspired by, and want to celebrate, the millions of people who have shown us that we can all have a positive impact.

Some people will tell you that there is no hope and that things will never change.

MY ANSWER IS THAT THERE WILL ALWAYS BE HOPE AS LONG AS THERE IS ACTION.

We don't have to witness the wrong in the world and assume someone else will fix it. We're not alone, and we can step up. It only takes a little push to get something big going.

If everyone does something, however small, we will all be part of a positive change in the world.

SO LET'S TURN THE NEGATIVE INTO POSITIVE!

May the good news begin

→

Through a sustained public commitment, Costa Rica has increased the size of its rainforests by 52% since 1984, which gives us hope for the Amazon. Change can happen!

More than 20 African countries have joined together to plant an 8,000 km-long wall of trees to restore the landscape and to stop the spread of the Sahara Desert.

People in a North Indian village knit giant sweaters for Indian elephants to protect them from near-freezing temperatures.

San Francisco's Cuddle Club unites senior people and senior dogs who need companionship, exercise, and affection.

Italian students are now required
to study climate change and sustainability
throughout their time at school.

In Japan, abandoned golf courses are being turned into solar farms. One "updated" golf course now powers 12,000 homes.

A NASA satellite study has shown that the world is a greener place than it was 20 years ago, thanks in part to ambitious tree planting initiatives in India and China.

Start
a Ripple

Bad news dominates the headlines and can make us feel powerless.

Did you know that just three minutes of negative news leaves you 27% more likely to have a bad day? It's no wonder, given that bad news feeds our fear and anxiety.

HOW CAN WE OVERCOME FEAR?

THE POWER OF POSITIVITY

1

Turn off news alerts on your phone and only absorb news at set times of the day.

2

Kindness is contagious. Look for opportunities to connect with and to support people in your daily life, creating a ripple effect of happiness.

3

While you can't avoid negative events from happening, you can control the way you see them. Is that issue worth your energy?

4

Make a list of happy thoughts: good friends, food, pets, and more. Refer to your list of happy thoughts when you feel unhappy or unworthy.

A single dad has taken his son with cerebral palsy to over 1,200 heavy metal concerts since finding out how much the music genre comforted him.

A 25-year-old inventor from Kenya has invented smart gloves that translate sign language into speech to help him communicate with his deaf niece.

A supermarket in Thailand says
no to plastic packaging and instead
wraps fresh produce in banana leaves.

Humpback whales have come back from the brink of extinction. Thanks to conservation efforts, populations have risen from hundreds to 25,000!

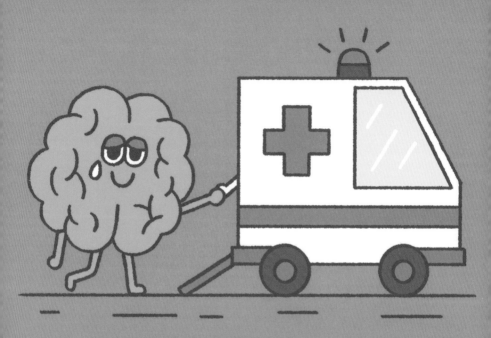

After it was revealed that more than 1,500 people die by suicide each year in Sweden, the country has premiered the world's first mental health ambulance.

Scientists have discovered a species of edible mushroom, *Pestalotiopsis microspora*, that consumes plastic. Landfill sites could be replaced with fungi-focused composting hubs.

To offset the erosion caused by flooding in Assam, India, a man planted a tree every day for 35 years, creating a forest larger than Central Park.

Green
is Good

They may not move, or talk, but trees are an incredible living presence in our daily lives.

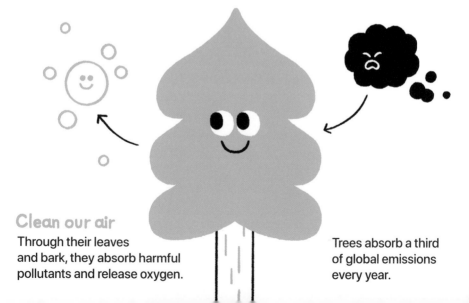

Clean our air

Through their leaves and bark, they absorb harmful pollutants and release oxygen.

Trees absorb a third of global emissions every year.

Regulate our climate

Trees help to cool down the planet and can reduce the overall temperature by up to 8°C.

Provide food

Trees provide food in the form of fruits, nuts, leaves, bark, and roots. Even dead trees provide food for insects.

Encourage biodiversity

Many birds, animals, and insects call trees home and use them for food, shelter, and protection.

Make us happy

A tree provides a great place to climb and explore. Trees like to be hugged!

STAND UP FOR TREES

Trees need us too

Speak up to save a mature tree

If you see a tree being cut down, find out why. If there isn't a good reason, start a local petition, or reach out to your council member.

Plant a tree

Participate in a volunteer planting day in your area. The best time of year for planting your tree is from October until March. This is because, like us, trees like to hibernate during winter.

Be a responsible paper user

Stop using paper towels and napkins, refuse paper bags, use recycled paper, and buy sustainably sourced wood products.

Defend the world's forests

Donate to support not-for-profit organizations that stand up for trees and take real action to stop forest loss, often by supporting local and indigenous communities.

DID YOU KNOW?

Beef products take a massive toll on trees. Especially in the Amazon, forests are being destroyed to clear the way for cattle ranches. Eating local, sustainably sourced beef from small farmers is the best way to ensure your beef consumption is also forest-friendly.

Scientists successfully reproduced endangered coral in a laboratory setting for the first time: a breakthrough that could potentially save our reefs!

Scientists have created a new way to edit DNA, called prime editing. It could fix up to 89% of the 75,000 genetic diseases we know about.

The Spanish company Ingelia have found a way to produce fuel without emitting any CO_2—by burning sewage!

NASA-inspired company Solar Foods wants to feed 9 billion people with food made from air: a protein powder created from captured CO_2.

In the last five years, Kenya's poaching rates have dropped by 85% for rhinos and 78% for elephants.

In Nepal, the number of tigers
in the wild has almost doubled
in under a decade.

A newspaper in Japan is made of recycled paper and seeds. Finished reading? Simply tear it into small pieces, plant it, and flowers will bloom!

After Australian bushfires, people from all over the world knitted little mittens for koalas with burnt paws, which raised almost $2 million in aid.

The 2017 women's marches were one of the largest—if not the largest—protests in American history, drawing crowds of more than 4 million nationwide.

Every Voice Counts

SPEAK UP!

Without people speaking up about what's important to them, things will never change.

 Make a sign and make it visible.

→ Volunteer with an organization working on something you care about.

→ Start a book club.

→ Write to your government representatives.

→ Talk to your friends and family about issues that are important.

It's easy to get disheartened by what we can't control, so focus on what you can do in your own family and community, and remember the power of one!

To prevent wildfires, the Portuguese government brought in herds of goats to manage thick undergrowth by doing what they do best: munch!

Canada has created an Arctic conservation zone almost as big as Germany to protect its sea birds, whales, and polar bears.

Seven eggs from the world's last two remaining northern white rhinoceroses were successfully fertilized in 2019. This may save the species!

Waste processing plants in China
are using up to 1 billion cockroaches to
process 50 tons of food waste per day.

Rice farmers around the world are using ducks instead of harmful pesticides! Ducks feed on insects and weeds without touching the plants.

In 2019, Norway adopted legislation to ban new fur farming operations, and to phase out the industry by 2025, joining many other European countries.

California became the first U.S. state to prohibit the sale of dogs, cats, and rabbits in pet stores unless the animals are from a rescue organization.

The Italian town of Collecchio, Parma, only allows silent fireworks, to alleviate pet stress and anxiety.

During the Covid-19 outbreak, people turned to dogs, cats, and chickens to cope with self-isolation. Many animal shelters emptied as all their animals were adopted.

Friendship is Golden

Doctors agree: <u>pets are good for us.</u>

If you have pets you already know the joy and love they bring to your life. Now science is confirming just how good they really are for you. How do they help?

Keep us active

Help socialize with other humans

Reduce stress and loneliness

Help us have empathy for others

Dogs alone have many jobs that are incredibly useful to us:

DID YOU KNOW?

Animal Assisted Therapy is a growing field that partners animals with people to help them recover from health problems, such as heart disease, cancer, and mental health conditions.

BEST FRIENDS

Being an animal shelter volunteer is good for your emotional, physical, and mental health.

It is scientifically proven that spending time with animals helps lower your stress levels and blood pressure. It will also keep you active, especially if you can walk a dog (or three)!

If you love animals, becoming a volunteer at your local shelter is definitely something you should consider.

Bring in Supplies

Donating goods and supplies can be a great way to serve local shelters. Most shelters have lists of items they need in order to keep the animals and facilities running.

Walking shelter dogs

Shelter dogs are kept inside for most of the day so will enjoy a long walk outside.

SOME WAYS YOU CAN HELP

Be a shelter photographer

A photograph makes a huge difference in how animals are perceived by potential adopters. One of the best ways you can volunteer is by taking photos of homeless pets.

Fostering a shelter animal

You can become an animal's temporary family for a few weeks until they get adopted.

You will be making a difference not only to the animals that reside there, but to the shelter, and to your community.

An international team of chemists have developed a technique to turn nearly a quarter of our plastic waste into fuel.

In the Netherlands five artificial islands
have been built to preserve wildlife. More
than 30,000 birds and 127 varieties
of plants have been reintroduced.

Germany is turning 62 decommissioned military bases into wildlife sanctuaries. This will increase Germany's area of protected wildlife by a quarter.

With the lowest prison population in Europe, Dutch prisons are being converted into housing for refugees.

Two companies in London and Vienna
are turning leftover bread into beer
to fight food waste.

Tattooing fruits and vegetables with lasers rather than using plastic stickers is changing the face of fruit labelling.

Sweden's blood donors receive
a text message whenever their
blood saves a life.

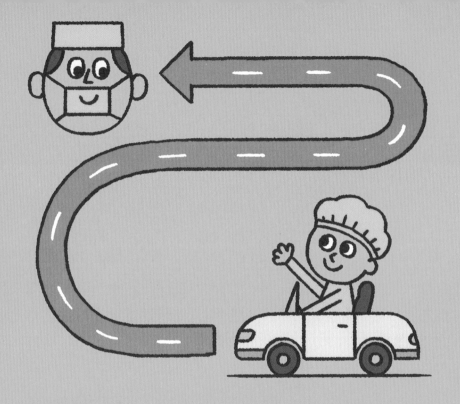

A Californian hospital rolled out a way to relieve kids' anxiety about surgery: they gave them mini-cars to drive themselves to their operations!

India has just launched its very first
Garbage Cafe, which provides food in exchange
for rubbish. This is a unique solution for
two issues: hunger and plastic waste.

Love What You Have

ZERO WASTE KIT

It is easy to be overwhelmed by the sheer volume of waste in our modern world. So concentrate on what you can control. You and the environment around you will be happier.

Instead of accepting plastic and styrofoam bags or cups, take your own containers with you. Limit fast food orders, and cook for yourself or go out to eat: both are more fun and rewarding.

Build a ZERO WASTE KIT that enables you to refuse plastic and paper as part of your daily routine.

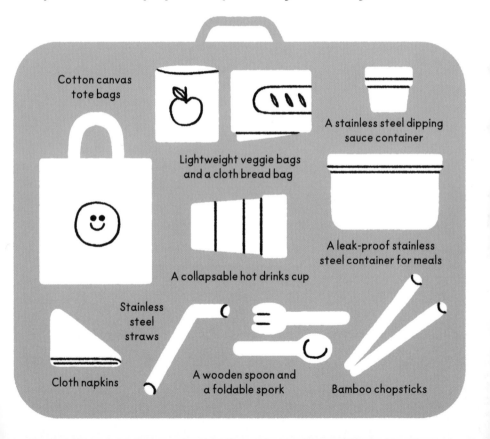

Cotton canvas
tote bags

Lightweight veggie bags
and a cloth bread bag

A stainless steel dipping
sauce container

A collapsable hot drinks cup

A leak-proof stainless
steel container for meals

Stainless
steel
straws

Cloth napkins

A wooden spoon and
a foldable spork

Bamboo chopsticks

The Netherlands has officially become
the first country without stray dogs, thanks
to its extensive animal welfare system.

The Billion Oyster Project is bringing back New York Harbor's long-lost oyster reefs, which will reduce water pollution and promote biodiversity.

Progress on gay rights is real.
Out of 195 countries in the world today,
128 have decriminalized homosexuality.

Scientists have successfully grown and harvested rice in the deserts of Dubai, an innovation which could help feed millions.

The Florida-based Saltwater Brewery has created edible six-pack rings that feed turtles and other marine creatures instead of harming them.

Dozens of countries came together and voted to ban the sale of wild baby African elephants to zoos and circuses around the world.

A blind inventor has revolutionized the walking stick by developing Smart Cane, which uses Google Maps and ultrasonic sensors to identify surroundings.

As the war raged in Syria and cat owners fled
the city, one man stayed behind and fed 170 cats.
His new nickname: The Cat Man of Aleppo.

Fabrics that can suck CO2 from the atmosphere are coming! A T-shirt made with living algae can generate as much oxygen as a six-year-old oak tree.

Dress
Responsibly!

Feeling comfortable with what we wear on
the outside makes us feel genuine
and positive on the inside.

The world consumes an astonishing 80 billion pieces of clothing annually and fast fashion comes at a huge cost to the environment! Avoid fast fashion, which is cheap, rapidly made clothing mass-produced in response to fads and trends.

When you buy new stuff, look for brands that:

Don't exploit overseas workers and pay living wages.

Use sustainable fabrics like cotton or recycled materials.

Minimize the use of chemicals.

Believe in upcycling (use discarded materials to make new products.)

And most importantly: buy less new stuff, and wear the clothes you love longer.

The incredible village of Piplantri in India celebrates their daughters by planting 111 trees every time a girl is born. So far they have planted more than 350,000 trees!

Saudi Arabia's ban on women driving officially ended in 2018. For the first time in history, Saudi Arabia's women were able to get behind the wheel.

Diego, a 100-year-old giant Galápagos tortoise, saved his species from extinction due to his "exceptional sex drive". He fathered an estimated 800 giant tortoises!

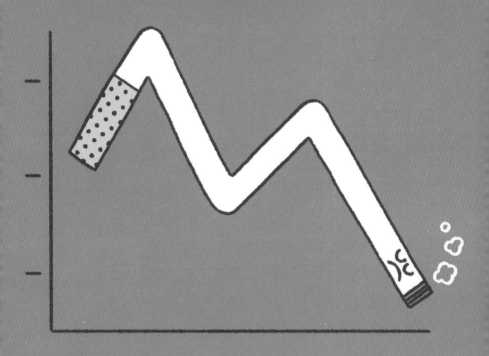

Tobacco smoking worldwide continues to decrease as fewer people, particularly fewer women, take up the habit.

By law in the Philippines, a graduating student must plant at least ten trees before receiving a diploma.

Giant Pandas are no longer endangered and China is going to build a massive panda conservation park worth $1.5 billion.

The city of Vienna will start rewarding concert and museum tickets to citizens who take public transport, cycle, or walk instead of driving.

Average global life expectancy
was just over 52 years in 1960.
It has now increased to 72 years.

Plastic-chomping caterpillars can help
fight plastic waste! Research shows that these
tiny mealworms can consume plastic without
it leaving residue in their bodies.

Squash the Food Footprint

The carbon footprint of food is the amount of greenhouse gas emitted during the growing, rearing, farming, processing, transporting, storing, cooking, and disposing of the food we eat.

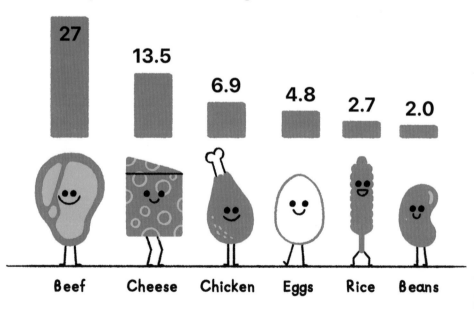

Kilograms of greenhouse gases per serving

Making modest adjustments to the food you eat can have a big impact, including:

 Reducing pollution

 Preserving the environment

 Slowing global warming

SOME SIMPLE TIPS

 Meat, especially beef and lamb, has a huge carbon footprint so eat less of it.

 Find protein alternatives and save your meat consumption for special occasions.

 As much as possible, buy all your meat and dairy from local small producers, which are available at most farmer's markets.

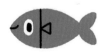 Make sure you are eating sustainably harvested or farmed fish.

Research has found that feeding seaweed to cows cuts 99% of greenhouse gas emissions from their burps and farts.

France was the first country to ban supermarkets from throwing away excess food. They must donate unused food or face a fine.

Scientists have discovered clean ice just below Mars' surface, which boosts hope for life there.

India is tackling its plastic waste problem by using plastic found in the Indian Ocean to build roads.

In Rome, people can pay for metro train tickets with plastic bottles, and hundreds of thousands of bottles have been recycled as a result!

In 2018, Iceland became the first country in the world to legally enforce equal pay for women and men.

The Ocean Cleanup Project launched a giant
U-shaped arm to capture rubbish in The Great
Pacific Garbage Patch (a floating mass
of debris twice the size of Texas).

The land iguana made its triumphant return
to the Galápagos island of Santiago thanks to
a large-scale reintroduction effort—200 years
after Charles Darwin's last official sighting.

In 2019, 633 divers set the Guinness World Record in Florida for the largest ocean underwater cleanup.

Nature Needs Us

BEACH CLEANUP

More and more waste, especially plastic, is finding its way into our oceans. It's harmful to ocean ecosystems all over the world, especially to sea life, from fish and whales to turtles and birds, who mistake the plastic for food.

Every year, beach cleanups are organized to help remove tons (yes, tons!) of trash, helping oceans stay cleaner and healthier.

If you live near a beach, go clean it*

*If you don't live near an ocean, chances are you may live near a river, lake, or stream that could you use your help.

cigarette butts

straws

THE **TOP** 6 ITEMS RECOVERED

food wrappers

plastic bottle caps

plastic bags

beverage cans and bottles

The death rate from cancer in the U.S. has hit
a milestone. It has been falling for
at least 25 years.

Holland covers its hundreds of bus stop shelters with plants. Known as "green roofs", these are ideal places for bees to take refuge.

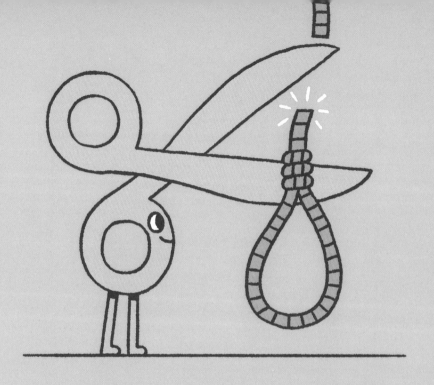

The global suicide rate has dropped by over 35% from its peak in 1994, saving over 4 million lives.

New Zealand's gun buy-back initiative
resulted in 10,000 banned firearms being taken
out of circulation in less than a month.

A dying dad found his match for a kidney transplant. He wore a T-shirt saying "In need of a kidney" on a family holiday to Disney World.

A robot called LarvalBot is delivering coral babies to the Great Barrier Reef to help restore the reefs to what they were.

The city of Las Vegas is testing an initiative that allows people to pay for parking tickets with a food donation.

British seagrass could help tackle climate change. The aquatic plant stores carbon 35 times more efficiently than tropical rainforests.

New research shows that bees love cannabis plants, which could help restore their dwindling populations.

Bee
Buddies

B E E S

Bees are the top pollinators for our planet, which means that they keep plants and crops alive and help them to reproduce.

Bees are responsible for helping farmers grow up to a third of the fruits and vegetables we eat. But bee colonies are in decline due to pesticides, pollution, and other factors.

The good news is that we can help!

Bee Bath

Fill a shallow container with water and pebbles for bees to land on.

Landing Pad

Plant bee-friendly flowers such as daisies and marigolds.

LET'S BUILD A BEE GARDEN!

Shelter

Bees appreciate protection from the elements, just like us. A simple way to create a shelter is to drill holes into a wooden block.

Bike-sharing is taking off around the world. Over the last decade, more than 1,000 cities have introduced bike-sharing.

A scientist has created fake plastic
from cactus juice that biodegrades in a
month and is safe to ingest.

In a new law passed by parliament, Portugal will have banned the use of wild animals in circuses by 2024.

With millennials leading the charge, plant-based diets continue to catch on across the world and are becoming part of mainstream culture.

Some 3,000 kg of rubbish has been collected from the Himalayas. Nepal's clean-up campaign is gathering momentum.

Soft drink sales in the U.S. dropped for the twelfth year in a row thanks to consumer education and new sugar taxes.

Whale sightings in New York City waters have increased by 540% since 2010, from 5 to 272, thanks to the success of environmental policies.

One and a half million volunteers in the Indian state of Madhya Pradesh set a new world record: they planted 66 million trees in just 12 hours.

Once a year, Berlin's unwanted Christmas
trees are used as food for zoo elephants.

Love Our Earth

Compost is organic material, such as food and outdoor waste, that can be added to soil to help plants grow.

WHY COMPOST?

Landfills will release less methane (a greenhouse gas).

Your soil will be enriched and retain more moisture.

It will help you to avoid using chemical fertilizers.

You will reduce your carbon footprint.

Follow these three basic steps to create nutrient-rich compost in a matter of weeks, either indoors or outdoors, for both large gardens and potted plants:

Add an equal amount of greens...
(grass clippings, vegetable or fruit waste)

and browns...
(dead leaves, branches, twigs, even paper towels)

And make sure moisture is present.

According to the Environmental Protection Agency (EPA), food scraps and outdoor waste make up 28% of what we throw away.

Julia, the *Sesame Street* character with autism, can help parents spot the signs of autism in their children at a younger age.

In its annual AIDS report, the United Nations noted that HIV-related deaths have dropped 33% since 2010.

The #FridaysForFuture movement was started by Greta Thunberg in 2018. Students from over 7,000 cities in 228 countries now protest against lack of action on the climate crisis.

Bhutan is the world's first carbon negative country, dedicating 72% of its land to forests, and committing to extensive climate change policies.

Australian surfers and activists continue to defeat multinational oil giants, forcing them to abandon plans to drill for oil in the Great Australian Bight.

In order to boost bee populations in the U.K., Backyard Nature gave away 15 million bee-friendly wildflower seeds to customers in supermarkets.

Canadian startup Carbon Engineering is building a facility that will be able to scrub a megaton of CO2 from the atmosphere annually.

California is the first state to have
banned the testing of beauty products
on animals.

In 2019, carbon emission levels in the U.K. went down for the sixth year in a row. Emission levels this low were last seen in 1888.

In a shift toward greener technology, British cities are getting air-filtering buses that suck pollution from the air.

Scotland produced enough wind energy to power all of its homes twice in the first half of 2019.

Stay Cool

Climate change can really impact our mental health, but we are in control of how we respond to it.

We still have a chance to act and preserve the planet for the next generation.

It's okay to feel stressed about climate change!

Change takes time but it also takes people like YOU.

Action, big or small, eases anxiety and it matters!

Here are some tips to help you cope with anxiety.

→ Advocate change

If you say you care about the planet, make sure your lifestyle reflects it. Use clean energy, buy local food when possible, eat less meat, and use public transportation.

→ Talk to others and take action

We need to unite to have a real impact. Chat with a trusted friend or family member who shares your values and concerns about the environment.

→ There are many not-for-profit organizations working on climate change that need your support.

The world's largest organic rooftop farm, around 14,000 sq m, will open in the heart of Paris in 2020.

Thanks, in a large way, to investment from China, it is estimated that the world's solar power capacity will triple by 2022.

Literacy rates continue to rise
from one generation to the next
and have reached an all-time high.

The world's first train lines powered directly by solar energy are set to launch in the U.K soon.

Nearly 1.2 billion people around the world have gained access to electricity over the last 16 years.

Breast cancer mortality has been declining for decades, with more than 375,000 lives saved since 1989.

According to UNESCO, more girls are in school than ever. The amount of girls starting primary education has increased by 25% in 40 years.

From Buckingham Palace in England to the beaches of Malibu, California, the ban on single-use plastic straws is expanding.

New Zealand has passed a bill to cut carbon
emissions to zero, plant 1 billion trees in the next
decade, and run its grid entirely from clean energy.

Underwater speakers are used to play the sounds of a vibrant living reef to attract young fish and to revitalize coral reefs.

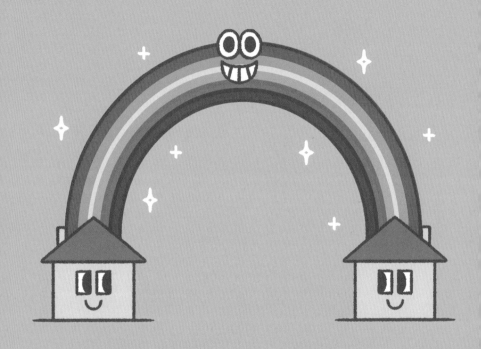

During the coronavirus pandemic, kids worldwide put rainbow pictures on their windows to spread a simple message: after every storm comes a rainbow.

Kindness is Contagious

It may seem like a small gesture, but positive sticky notes can have a huge impact on someone's day.

 1

 **2**

Get a sticky note.

Fill it with a drawing and/or a positive message.

My advice: don't spend too much time on a note, it has to feel genuine and authentic.

3

Stick it up in a public place (anonymously)... ↘

... on a parked car, a house door, dressing rooms, bathroom mirrors, city benches, a friend's computer...

... anywhere that needs a little kindness!

I like to stick my notes by the lift or elevator to add a little bit of happiness whether someone is coming or going!

We're often so caught up with our busy schedules that we don't naturally reach out to do something positive with our friends—or with strangers.

Carrying out one random act of kindness per week dramatically improves your happiness.

You hold the power to make someone's day with a small, but selfless, act.

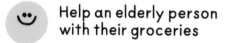 Help an elderly person with their groceries

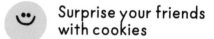 Surprise your friends with cookies

😊 Pay it backward: buy coffee for the person behind you in line

😊 Check in on your friends to make sure they're ok

😊 Donate used books to the local library

😊 Smile at people (even if you feel grouchy)

😊 Return bags and trollies at food stores

😊 Put your phone away while in the company of others

You can start small, and after a while, you'll find yourself being kind without even thinking about it.

As millions of people have demonstrated,
change is possible, solutions are out there,
and a better world and future can be built.

ONE STEP AT A TIME, WE CAN ALL HAVE A POSITIVE IMPACT!

Goodbye

About Mauro

Originally from Italy, Mauro Gatti lives in Los Angeles where everyone surfs except him. Mauro is an award-winning creative director, illustrator, and designer who loves pizza, dogs, and imagining things. He also loves to make people happy with his art, because a smile is the cheapest route to happiness.

@the_happy_broadcast   @happybcast   @thehappybroadcast